THE YUK FACTOR

Contents

Keep It Clean! page 2

The Dirt Busters page 16

Haydn Middleton

Story illustrated by
Dan Chernett

Heinemann

Find out about

- How to stay healthy and avoid Athlete's Foot, cold viruses and bad bacteria

Tricky words

- billions
- creatures
- asthma
- fungi
- sweaty
- Athlete's Foot
- viruses
- bacteria

Introduce these tricky words and help the reader when they come across them later!

Text starter

All around you there are billions of tiny creatures that are too small to see, like dust mites, fungi, viruses and bacteria. Some of them are friendly. But some are not so friendly – dust mite poo can cause asthma and fungi can cause Athlete's Foot. How can you avoid these unfriendly creatures?

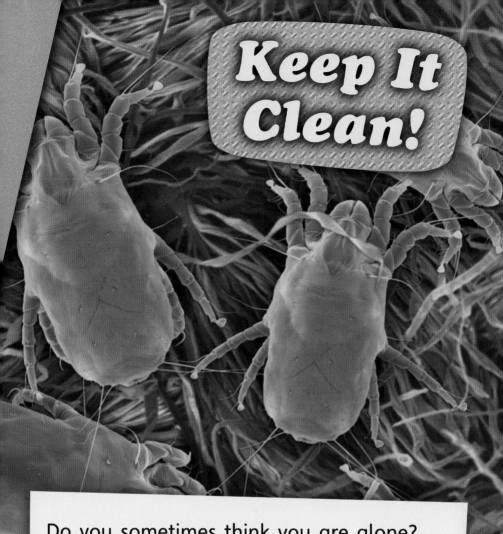

Keep It Clean!

Do you sometimes think you are alone? Well, you are not. Billions of tiny creatures are all around you, but they are too small to see. Some of these tiny creatures are friendly to your body and some are not so friendly.

Dust mites

Dust mites chomp on tiny flakes of
dead skin that fall off you all the time.
Dust mites live all over your house,
but they really like carpets, mattresses
and pillows.
Dust mites are not friendly to your body.

Dust mites are
microscopic - 50 could
fit on the head of a pin!

Dust mites poo a lot, and that can be a problem if you suffer from asthma.

You might find it hard to breathe and have an asthma attack.

If you hoover your carpets and wash your sheets and pillowcases a lot, you will have fewer dust mites.

Fungi

Some tiny creatures feed on your skin *before* it flakes off. These creatures are called fungi.

Fungi love to nibble on dead skin between your toes when your feet are wet or sweaty. If you walk around with bare feet you leave fungi on the floor that can infect someone else's bare feet.

Fungi are not friendly to your body.

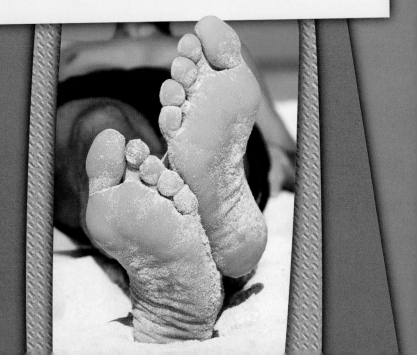

The fungi can leave an itchy rash on your skin. This rash is called Athlete's Foot. Here's how to avoid Athlete's Foot:

- Wash your feet often.
- Dry your feet carefully.
- Don't wear tight trainers – they make your feet sweat.
- Change your socks often.
- Don't wear anyone else's socks – Athlete's Foot is catching!

cold virus

Viruses

If you have a cold you may sneeze a lot. What comes out of your nose when you sneeze? Snot!

But not just snot. You also send billions of viruses into the air – at more than 60 miles an hour!

Viruses are not friendly to your body.

Other people breathe in the viruses.

Then *they* begin to sneeze!

People can also catch your cold if they touch something you have touched and then they touch their nose or mouth.

Here's how to avoid catching a cold:

- Wash your hands a lot.

- Eat healthy food.

- Get lots of sleep.

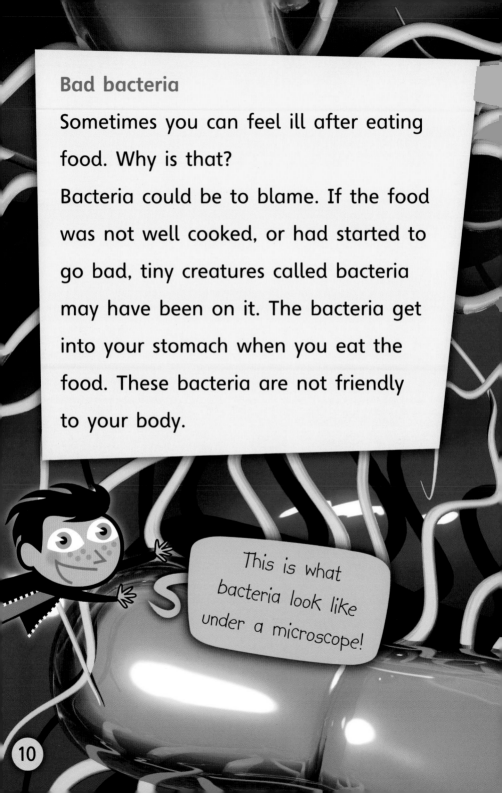

Bad bacteria

Sometimes you can feel ill after eating food. Why is that?

Bacteria could be to blame. If the food was not well cooked, or had started to go bad, tiny creatures called bacteria may have been on it. The bacteria get into your stomach when you eat the food. These bacteria are not friendly to your body.

This is what bacteria look like under a microscope!

Here's how to prevent your food from making you ill:

- Make sure meat is well cooked to kill off the bacteria.
- Wash your hands before and after touching raw meat.
- Wash fruit and vegetables.
- Make sure food hasn't been left out of the fridge too long, and isn't past its sell-by date.

Good bacteria

Not all bacteria are bad for your body.

Some bacteria are good for you.

Good bacteria live in your stomach and help you to digest your food.

Some foods, like cheese and yoghurt, have good bacteria in them.

good bacteria

Here's how to help your body stay healthy:

- Eat foods with good bacteria, like cheese and yoghurt.
- Keep your fingernails clean and wash your hands before eating to stop bad bacteria getting into your food.
- Brush your teeth and your tongue to stop bad bacteria from causing bad breath and gum disease.

There are billions of tiny creatures living all around you, even if you can't see them. Some are friendly and help to keep you well. But some are unfriendly and make you ill. So the next time you think you are all alone just remember – you are *not!*

Quiz

Text Detective

- What can you do to stop the spread of Athlete's Foot?
- How would you tell a friend to keep healthy?

Word Detective

- **Phonic Focus:** Identifying phonemes in complex words
  Page 7: How many syllables are there in 'avoid'?
  What is the vowel phoneme in each syllable?
- Page 7: Can you find a compound word on this page?
- Page 12: Find two words that are opposite in meaning.

Super Speller

Read these words:

before   touched   friendly

Now try to spell them!

HA! HA! HA!

Q If a fly and a flea pass each other what time is it?

A Fly past flea!

In this story

 Josh

 Josh's mum

 Lindy

 Sue

Tricky words

- earphones
- filthy
- wondered
- wrinkled
- gasped
- sandwich
- mould
- cameraman

Introduce these tricky words and help the reader when they come across them later!

Story starter

Josh spends so much time watching TV he never gets round to tidying his bedroom. One evening he was watching *Dirt Busters*, a programme where Lindy and Sue turn up at people's houses to find out how clean their rooms are.

The Dirt Busters

"I can't find the earphones for my MP3 player!" Josh told his mum.

"Look for them in that filthy room of yours!" she said.

"But I'm watching TV," said Josh.

"You're **always** watching TV," said his mum.

Dirt Busters was on the TV, and Josh wondered whose room Lindy and Sue would inspect today. They were looking for the house right now. "Mum is wrong about my room," Josh thought. "It might be a bit untidy, but it's not *that* bad."

Josh looked at the house Lindy and Sue were about to go into on the TV.

"Hey, that's *my* house!" Josh cried.

He blinked. The TV seemed to be coming closer. He blinked again. No, he was getting closer to the TV. He was being sucked inside the screen!

Josh found himself at his front door.

He was letting Lindy and Sue into his house.

"Right, Josh," said Lindy, rubbing her hands in her rubber gloves.

"Take us to your room," said Sue.

"It's time to inspect!"

Josh led the way up the stairs.
Already he could smell his room.
Sue wrinkled her nose in disgust.
"Wow, what a stink!" she said. "And
we're not even inside yet!"
"I bet he never opens his window,"
said Lindy.

It was difficult to open the door because there was stuff all over the floor.

"What a mess!" gasped Lindy. "And it looks filthy!"

"It may be untidy," said Josh, "but it's **not** filthy!"

"Really?" laughed Sue. "What's all this then?"

Does Josh's room look filthy to you?

She stamped across Josh's comics and
pointed at a mass of cobwebs.

"**Not** very clean," she said.

"Yes, but they're clean spiders," said Josh.

"And how about all those dead flies?"
asked Lindy. "Are they clean too?"

"No," said Josh quietly.

Sue picked something off the carpet.
"Yuk!" she said. "A smelly football sock!"
"It's only a bit smelly," said Josh.
"Your dirty clothes are all mixed up
with your clean clothes," said Sue as
she threw the smelly sock at Josh.

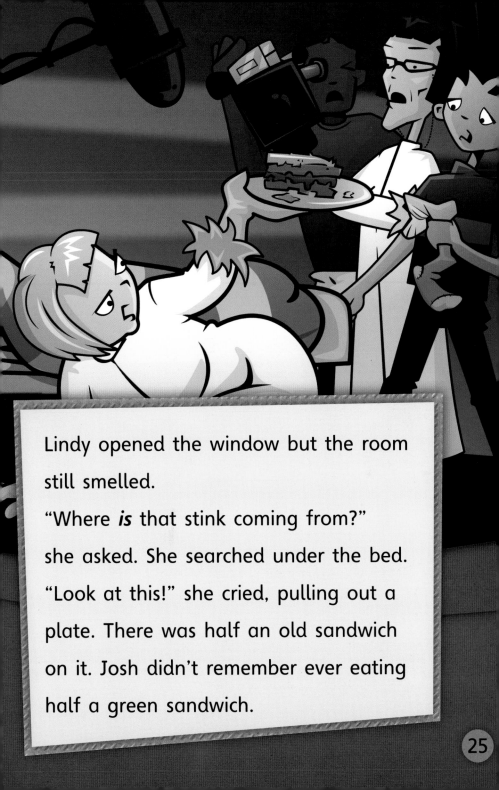

Lindy opened the window but the room still smelled.

"Where *is* that stink coming from?" she asked. She searched under the bed.

"Look at this!" she cried, pulling out a plate. There was half an old sandwich on it. Josh didn't remember ever eating half a green sandwich.

"This bread is covered in mould!" said
Lindy with a shiver. "You know what
mould is, don't you?"

"I suppose it's something nasty," said Josh.

"It's a *fungus!*" Sue yelled in his ear.

Lindy pulled another plate out from under a pile of shirts.

"How long has *that* been there?" Sue demanded.

"Oh," said Josh, looking at the mess on the plate, "I'm not too sure."

The cameraman did a close-up on the plate.

Can you tell what is on the plate?

There was an old burger and a few old chips, but there was something else on top of the food. It was white and it was moving about.

"Yuk!" said Lindy. "Maggots!"

"Don't you **know** how stupid it is to let old food go bad in your room?" Sue yelled at Josh. "Do you **like** maggots?"

"No," said Josh, "they are disgusting." He looked at the maggots crawling on the plate.

"No, **you** are disgusting!" shouted Sue.

Then ... *ZAP!* It all went dark.

Josh found himself back on his sofa.

He was holding his smelly football sock.

There seemed to be something inside it.

"Oh no," he thought, "is it maggots?"

But when he looked inside, he saw ...

his lost earphones!

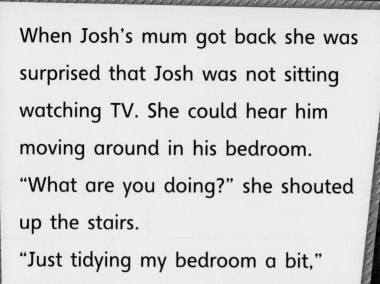

When Josh's mum got back she was surprised that Josh was not sitting watching TV. She could hear him moving around in his bedroom.

"What are you doing?" she shouted up the stairs.

"Just tidying my bedroom a bit," called Josh.

Quiz

Text Detective

- What did Lindy and Sue find in Josh's room?
- Why do you think Josh was tidying his room at the end?

Word Detective

- **Phonic Focus:** Identifying phonemes in complex words
  Page 29: How many syllables are there in 'disgusting'?
  What is the vowel phoneme in each syllable?
- Page 24: Find two words that are opposite in meaning.
- Page 29: Find a word that means 'foolish'.

Super Speller

Read these words:

wrong   about   already

Now try to spell them!

HA! HA! HA!

Q How many burgers can you eat on an empty stomach?

A One – after that your stomach's not empty!